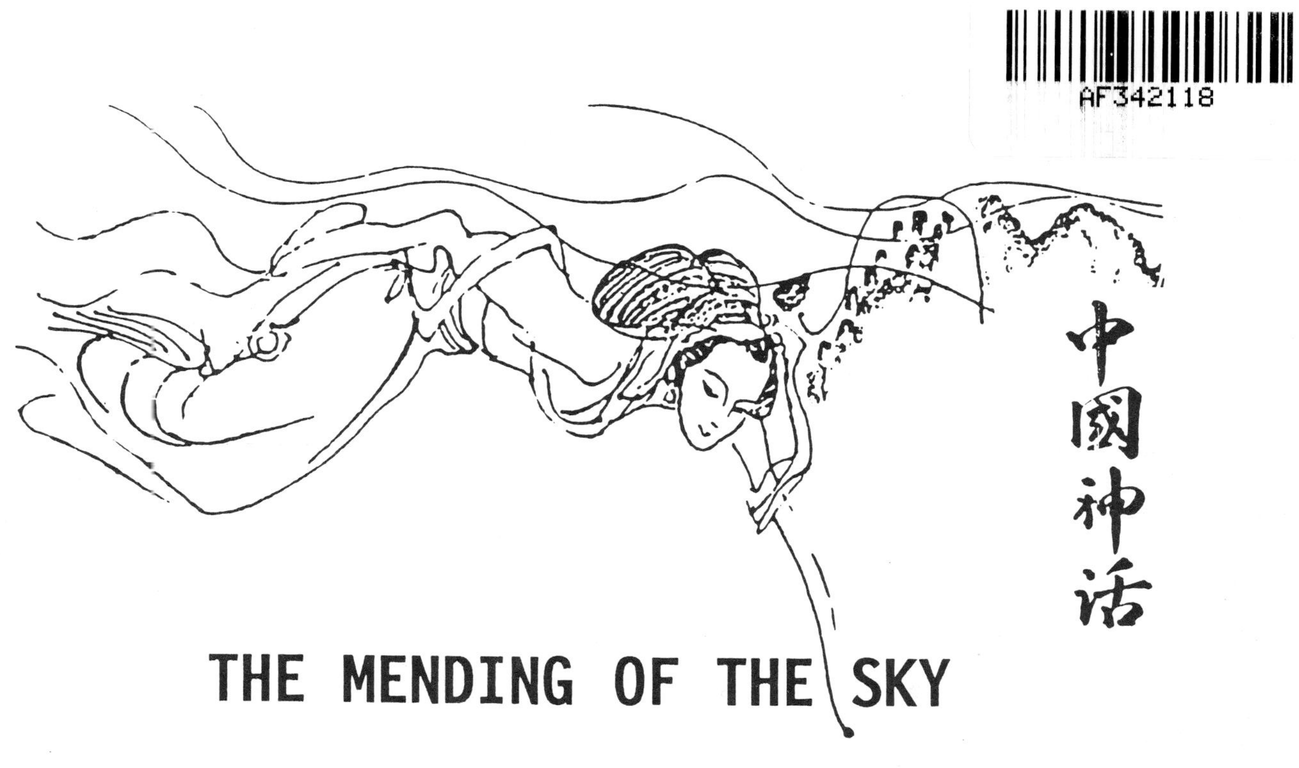

THE MENDING OF THE SKY

AND OTHER CHINESE MYTHS

Retold by Li Xiao Ming

Illustrations from Wu Shan Ming

Oyster River Press

ISBN 0 9617481 3 3

Translations by Li Xiao Ming

Illustrations from Wu Shan Ming
Calligraphy by Xu Peng

Thanks to Zhang Rong Yan,
for her good counsel

Book Design by Cicely Buckley

Published by the Oyster River Press
20 Riverview Road, Durham, NH 03924

CONTENTS

Introduction

The origin of human life is attributed to the goddess Nü Wa, who created figures of yellow clay to overcome her boredom. Her way was prepared by the early ordering of the universe, when one god separated sky and earth. Another destroyed nine of the ten suns that threatened to scorch the earth. The people were saved again from disaster when the Yellow Dragon used good engineering to divert the waters of a great flood.

Gods, demi-gods and emperors (or emperors who were believed to be gods, some with the attributes of the animals) vied for power over earth and heaven, calling on the spirits of rain and wind to assist them. They fought bloody battles to establish their hegemony. Others earned respect and godliness when they sacrificed themselves in the discovery of pottery, silk and the use of herbs for medicine.

These myths are told today as examples of human ingenuity and good conduct. Elders point out to children the bridge of stars in the great Silver River (Milky Way) where the daughter of the Heavenly Emperor meets yearly with her earthly husband, from whom she was forced to separate when it was learned she had betrothed a mortal. And a young woman found herself radically changed when she broke a promise made to her father's horse.

During the Sino-Japanese war of 1937-1945, Mao recalled the gods who intervened to help an old man who wanted to move mountains. "If we persist," said Mao, "one day we will move the people. With their support we can move mountains and defeat the invaders." His hope was realized when he found nationwide support to help defeat the Japanese in 1945. As new chapters are written in world history, we find inspiration from these ancient tales of human invention and sacrifice. C.B.

盘古开天地

I. PAN GU OPENED UP THE SKY AND THE EARTH

It is said that before the sky and earth were separate, there was chaos in the universe, and darkness, like the inside of a big egg. Our ancestor Pan Gu was born in the big egg. He slept there, growing and maturing, for eighteen thousand years. One day he awoke to find himself in utter darkness, unable to see anything in that sticky and suffocating world. He picked up his axe and swung it around him in the darkness, causing the big eggshell to break up with a thunderous noise. The light stuff in the egg rose up to become the sky; the heavy, dark stuff subsided to become the earth.

Fearing that the sky and earth would come together again, Pan Gu stood between them, his head propping up the sky, his feet pressing down on the earth. Every day he grew one zhang taller. (A zhang equals 3.333 meters). After another eighteen thousand years, Pan Gu was more than ninety li tall. (One li is O.5 kilometers.) Like a pillar he stood there for many years, exerting all his strength to prevent sky and earth from coming together again. Finally, exhausted, he fell down, dying.

His body underwent an amazing transformation. His breath became the wind and the clouds, his voice the rumbling thunder. His right eye became the sun, his left eye the moon. His body was changed into tall mountains, his blood into rivers, his tendons and sinews the roads, and his muscles, the soil. His hair and beard turned into the stars in the sky, his skin and the fine hair of his body into flowers, grass and foliage. His teeth and bones turned into shiny metals, hard rocks, precious pearls and jade. Even his perspiration became rain drops and morning dew. Every part of Pan Gu's body helped to make the world a better place for living.

II. NÜ WA CREATED HUMAN BEINGS

After the sky and earth were separated, although there were mountains and trees, and birds and fishes, the world still seemed bleak and desolate to the Goddess Nü Wa, who had a human head and the body of a serpent. She felt very lonely as she wandered about the world.

Sitting beside a pond, she dug up some yellow mud and kneeded it with water. Looking at her own reflection, she made a baby figure out of the mud. When the mud figure touched the ground, it began to move around, and called her "mama". She named the new life "Ren" which means human. Surprised and pleased with her first success, she made more mud figures. They came alive, danced and spoke cheerfully around her, then wandered away from her.

She wanted to fill the earth with these agile and joyful beings, so she worked for a long time until she was too tired to do more. Dipping a vine stalk into the same mud, she sprinkled the ground with it, and many more mud figures sprang from the ground where the mud fell.

Nü Wa understood that the new creatures were mortal and must die. So she matched male with female, in order that humans might reproduce themselves. In some parts of China, Nü Wa is worshipped as the first matchmaker, the goddess of marriage.

III. NÜ WA MENDED THE SKY

For many years after they were created by Nü Wa, humans lived happily. But one day a corner of the sky collapsed, and a part of the earth caved in. Forests in the mountains caught on fire, floods rose from under the ground, and animals, fleeing from the forests, began to attack people.

Nü Wa was alarmed that her children's lives were endangered. She decided to mend the sky. From the rivers she picked up five-colored rocks and boiled and melted them in a huge cauldron, then carried the liquid to the sky to patch up the hole. She then took the four legs of a huge tortoise as pillars to hold up the sky.

As soon as the sky was mended, the flood subsided, and the fires were extinguished. Humans once again lived happy and carefree, as Nü Wa quietly returned to heaven.

IV. FU XI TAUGHT PEOPLE TO USE FIRE

In the far corner of northern China, there was a pure land inhabited by gods on earth. One day a girl from that land went to the east, stopping by a scenic and lush marshland. By the side of a swamp, she discovered the footprint of a giant, overgrown with beautiful flowers. Full of curiosity, the girl from the pure land stepped into the giant's footstep, as something stirred inside her body. She became pregnant, and soon gave birth to a son called Fu Xi.

With his human head and body of a dragon, Fu Xi looked exactly like his father, the God of Thunder, who ruled the swampland. Fu Xi was endowed with superhuman powers. He could even travel between heaven and earth by way of the heavenly ladder, which according to the record was accessible only to gods, other immortals and sorcerers. (The sorcerers were those who brought the word of the deities to humans, and conveyed the mortals' complaints to the gods.)

Fu Xi was made Heavenly God of the East. With the assistance of the god of the woods, he was responsible for the yearly renewal of spring.

By striking the trees with his lightning, Fu Xi made fire. He invented the fishnet, and taught the people how to hunt and fish. He also taught them how to make camp fires to protect themselves from the attack of wild animals, and how to use fire for cooking.

V. EMPEROR SHUN, THE POPULAR MONARCH

In ancient times, China was inhabited by many nationalities, worshipping different gods. In the east, the "Yin" people worshipped Shun, one of their earliest rulers. Shun was unusual from birth.

One night, an old blind man had a strange dream. A phoenix appeared to tell him that he would have a son. A few days later, the old man's wife gave birth to a dark-skinned boy named Shun, who grew to medium height. Shun's eyes were unusual: each of his eyes had two pupils.

His mother died soon after his birth, and his stepmother disliked him. Although he tried his best to wait on his parents, she was never pleased. She gave him little to eat and often beat him. So Shun left home at an early age, to live alone in a hut at the foot of a mountain, close to a river. He sympathized with the unfortunate, who reminded him of his own experience.

He was an ingenious farmer, fisherman and pottery-maker. People liked him for his generosity and skills. In three years, his village developed to a sizeable town, and then became the main city of his country. At that time, the aged monarch Yao was looking for a successor.

All the tribes' leaders recommended Shun. The Emperor Yao gave him his two daughters in marriage and made him emperor of the land. Although Shun was now rich and powerful, he was also forgiving. He still treated his parents as a pious son, and his stepmother's heart was softened by his loyalty and kindness.

His accomplishments were many. Shun had performed the great sacrifices, had presented offerings to the mountains, examined the work of the feudal lords when he toured the four quarters every five years. He also corrected measurement standards, introduced penal codes and punished the wrongdoers.

大禹治水

VI. THE YELLOW DRAGON SUBDUED THE FLOOD

For more than twenty years, the great flood covered the earth. Da Yu, a fearless yellow dragon with two hard horns, leading a host of other dragons, came down to earth to harness the flood and save the people.

He brought with him a special kind of soil from heaven, which could grow by itself when it touched the ground. With the help of a big black tortoise which carried his magic soil, the yellow dragon was able to level the lower plains and raise the places where people lived. And with the help of the other dragons, he channeled the waters into the East Sea. Today we see high mountains where he dumped most of the soil.

Sitting on a mountain peak, Da Yu was observing the course of the water of the Yellow River when suddenly an old man with a white face and the body of a fish jumped up from the river, claiming to be the spirit of the river. He gave Da Yu a bluish stone and disappeared. In the natural lines of the stone, Da Yu saw a map of the channels that would carry the flood waters to the sea. Using the map, his project proceeded smoothly.

Heaven had given him this Great Plan to help him, because he dug soil and led the rivers to the sea, without obstructing the natural elements by damming up the waters. To carry out the plan, he travelled to the four corners of the land.

In the East, he came upon the land of immortals, the place where the ten suns rested, bathed and from which they rose into the sky. In the far South was the land of red grain, boiling springs, laquer trees and the mountain of nine brilliances, the land of the winged people and the naked people. In the West he saw the wizard's mountain, the mountain of accumulated gold, the land of people who lived on air and morning dew, and of the people with three faces and one arm. In the North, in the countries of barbarians, he came upon the holy mountain, the accumulated waters and the mountain of piled up stones. He worked so hard that he did not see his family for ten long years.

As the waters subsided, a monster with a snakes's body and nine heads and mouths, all eating at the same time, caused the people much alarm. From its nine mouths gushed poisonous water, creating deep ponds, endangering the lives of people and animals. Da Yu, the fearless yellow dragon, killed the monster. Emperor Shun gladly made him his successor to the throne.

And if it were not for Da Yu who channeled the waters of the great flood, would we not all be fishes?

VII. THE EMPRESS XIANG BAMBOO

Emperor Shun, during his reign, cared deeply about the welfare of the people and enjoyed great popularity. He died of an illness while inspecting the southern part of the country. Everyone mourned his death, and his two wives were heartbroken.

On their way to the south, traveling along the Xiang Jiang River by boat, they wept the whole way. Their tears left indelible traces where they fell on the bamboo stalks. Today the local people call this special mottled bamboo the Empress Xiang Bamboo.

Unfortunately, before they reached their destination, the boat capsized in a big storm and the two empresses were drowned.

People believe they are now river spirits, haunting the site where they drowned. Some claim to have seen them in storms, still moaning for their beloved husband.

VIII. YI SHOT DOWN NINE SUNS

The Emperor of the Heavens had three wives, one of whom was the Sun Goddess. She gave birth to ten suns that took their places in the sky. Every day they would come out one by one. Later, because they did not want to wait their turn, they came out to shine all at once. As crops dried up, the earth was singed and people were dying of heat and starvation. The world turned into a kind of hell, unbearable for living.

The god Yi, saddened by what he saw, came down with his wife Chang E to save the people. He took his red bow and white arrow and shot at one of the suns. Those who looked closely at the flaming ball that fell to the ground saw that it was a colossal golden crow, with three feet, the spirit of the sun.

As the crowds cheered, Yi saw that nine suns remained in the sky. He shot eight more white arrows into the sky, one after another, eight more fire balls exploded and eight more three-footed golden crows lay on the ground. While the unbearable heat on earth subsided, Yi realized that the crops needed light and warmth to grow, so he left the last sun in the sky. The day was divided into day and night as the last sun rose and set in a regular rhythm.

IX. CHANG E RAN TO THE MOON

When Yi shot down the nine suns, although people were saved from disaster, the Emperor of the Heaven was offended, for Yi had killed nine of his sons. He sent Yi and his wife Chang E into exile on earth, where they became mortals and would never be able to return to heaven.

Hoping to regain his immortality, Yi went to Mount Kun Lun to request the medicine of longevity from the Mother of the Western King. Mount Kun Lun, the highest in the world, was surrounded by fire. Yet the brave Yi overcame all obstacles to meet the Mother of the King of the West. She admired his bravery and gave him the medicine, warning that if he and his wife took it, there would be enough for both of them to live forever. But if one should take it all, only that one might become a god again.

Yi entrusted the medicine to his wife, who was still regretting her husband's acts which forced them into exile. Eager to return to heaven, she secretly took all the medicine herself. All at once she lost control of her body and floated up to the sky. She dared not return to the heavenly court as a wife who had betrayed her husband, so went to the moon instead. The moon was a lonely place, with only one white rabbit for company, pounding medicine in a morter.

X. THE YAN EMPEROR, GOD OF AGRICULTURE

The Yan Emperor, God of the Sun, had the head of an ox and a human body. When he was born, nine wells appeared around him, all connected to each other. Water drawn from one would stir the water in all the others.

When he came down to earth, humans had multiplied to such an extent that the wild food they harvested was not enough to feed them. The Yan Emperor taught them how to grow their own food crops, like millet, wheat and beans. He also sent down more sunlight to warm the crops, and seeds showered down from the sky. These he gathered and sowed in the fields. He is remembered as the god of agriculture.

The Yan Emperor is also called the god of medicine, since the sun is believed to be the source of health. When he saw people suffering from pain and disease, he searched over all the mountains, tasting all the herbs to find those that would cure their ailments. He was poisoned a number of times, even in a single day. Luckily, he was always able to find an antidote to save himself from the effect of the poison.

By whipping the herbs with his divine whip, he could tell which were poisonous and which were beneficial. Some believed the whip was really his tongue, tasting every kind of herb to make sure it was not harmful as a remedy. But one day, he tasted a very poisonous herb which eroded his intestines, and died. Even today a special vine with yellow flowers is identified as the one that killed the Yan Emperor.

XI. JING WEI TRIED TO FILL UP THE SEA

The youngest daughter of the Yan Emperor was Baby Wa. One day Baby Wa went to the East Sea for her pleasure. Unfortunately, a violent sea storm raged there, and she drowned. Her spirit turned into a small bird, called Jing Wei.

Jing Wei, who looked like a crow with a spotted head, a white beak and red feet, lived on a northern mountain. Every day this little bird picked up small stones and branches and threw them into the East Sea.

The big ocean laughed at her, saying,

"Little bird, you won't be able to fill me up, even if you work for ten thousand years!"

Jing Wei circled around the sky, saying, "I would work a billion years to fill you up!"

The ocean asked her why that was so.

"To keep you from taking more lives," she replied.

It was believed that later on Jing Wei mated with a seagull; their female children grew up like Jing Wei, while their male children resembled the seagull. It was the task of the female birds to continue filling up the ocean.

瑶姬与神女峰

XII. YAO JI GUIDED THE BOATMEN

One of the Yan Emperor's daughters, Yao Ji, was returning from learning the divine skills from the East Sea. She lingered by the beautiful Wu Mountain. At that time, Da Yu was leading the people to harness the flood. Suddenly, a mighty wind came up, shaking the mountain and the plains, the rocks and trees. The Yellow Dragon sought help from Yao Ji.

Using her divine skills, the goddess Yao Ji appeased the wind. The channeling of the waters could be resumed, and the tunnel through Wu Mountain was successfully completed.

Having made friends with the local people, and fascinated by the Wu Mountain, Yao Ji was reluctant to leave and stayed on. Every day she stood on the top of the mountain to watch ships sail among the Three Gorges of the Yangtze River, the most dangerous waterway of the land. She was concerned about the safety of the boatmen, so sent hundreds of divine birds to guide them.

Standing there year after year, Yao Ji and her maidens gradually turned into mountain peaks; the seventy-two peaks of Wu Mountain are their remains. The most beautiful one is the goddess Yao Ji. Today as boatmen sail across the three gorges, they look up at Shen Nu Feng (the Peak of the Goddess) and remember Yao Ji.

寧封子造陶

XIII. NING FENG ZI MADE POTTERY

During the time of the great floods, people retreated to mountain caves, and went down daily to the overflowing rivers to fetch water. But their crude containers were easily broken.

Ning Feng Zi, an official of the Yellow Emperor, discovered one day while roasting animal meat that the earth burnt in the fire became hard and solid. Overjoyed, he built a kiln and set a fire on its top. But the fire was not burning well, so Ning Feng Zi jumped in to add fuel to the fire, which began to glow brighter. His figure could be seen floating up and down in the flames. Later, when the kiln was opened, his remains were found in the ashes. Ever since that time he has been remembered as the pottery god.

The pottery that came from that fire was the best ever seen, and proved to be of much better quality than the earthen jugs people had used before. Ning Feng Zi's remains were buried in Mount Qing Yuan, where his heroic sacrifice is still remembered.

XIV. THE YELLOW EMPEROR

The supreme ruler of heaven and earth was the Yellow Emperor, who had four faces, so that he could watch four directions at the same time. Under him were four divine emperors, each in charge of one part of the world and one season of the year.

The great Yellow Emperor would sit at the center of the heavenly court, attended by the god of earth, holding a rope in his hand. The Emperor of the East, Fu Xi, was in charge of spring. His assistant was the god of the woods, with a pair of compasses in his hand. The Emperor of the South, the Yan Emperor, was in charge of summer, assisted by the god of fire, who held the balancing scales.

The Emperor of the West was Shao Hao, responsible for autumn, with his assistant, the god of gold, who had a ruler in his hand. In charge of winter was the Emperor of the North, Zhuan Xu, assisted by the god of water, holding the sliding weight scales.

One day the Yellow Emperor went to Mount Tai to meet with all the gods of the universe. He traveled in a precious cart pulled by a great elephant, followed by six dragons. His general Chi You led packs of wild animals to open up the road for him. The god of the wind and the god of rain went along to clear the road of dust. Following the Emperor's cart came his subordinate emperors and all the rest of the gods.

黃帝征蚩尤

XV. THE WAR WITH CHI YOU

Before coming to the throne and establishing his position as supreme ruler, the Yellow Emperor first had to subdue his brother, the Yan Emperor. He was challenged by Chi You, who like his grandfather, the Yan Emperor, had the head of an ox and a human body. His seventy-two brothers, fierce-looking with their brass scalps and iron foreheads, had animal bodies, but spoke the language of humans.

After the Yan Emperor was defeated, Chi You served for a time as one of the Yellow Emperor's courageous generals. Yet he harbored the desire to avenge his grandfather, who thought he was too old to lead another war, and was content with what he had. So Chi You went to war in his name.

In several battles, the Yellow Emperor was defeated. Chi You had enlisted in his army some spirits from the mountains and swamps who made a very strange sound; when humans heard this sound, they felt dizzy, and followed the sound blindly into the enemy trap. Many of the Yellow Emperor's soldiers were killed in this way.

The Yellow Emperor found out that these spirits were afraid of the dragon's noise. So he ordered the soldiers to make bugles out of horns of oxen and goats, which sounded like the groaning of a dragon when they were blown at a low pitch. The spirits of the mountains and waters were scared and ran away.

Then the Yellow Emperor sent a real, divine dragon to pour torrents of water over Chi You's army and drown all the soldiers. But before the dragon arrived, Chi You invited the gods of wind and rain to make a mighty storm. The torrential storm forced the army of the Yellow Emperor to retreat.

XVI. WHY THE MAPLE LEAVES ARE RED

The Yellow Emperor was unable to fight back without the assistance of the goddess Xuan Nü, who had a human head but a bird's body. She helped him with her special divine skills and knowledge of war. She advised him to reposition his armies and to constantly change their distribution, to elude the enemy.

The Yellow Emperor also obtained red copper from Mount Kun Lun. He used it to manufacture double-edged swords, which were so sharp that they could cut jade as if they were cutting through mud.

Although Chi You and his brothers were strong and daring, they were inferior in tactics and weaponry. In the final showdown, Chi You was captured alive by the Yellow Emperor, who ordered his execution. But for fear of Chi You's supernatural strength, they bound him with fetters and shackles before killing him.

After his death, the blood-stained fetters were dismantled and thrown into the wasteland. When they touched the ground, they turned into a forest of maple trees, with crimson leaves, colored by the blood of Chi You.

XVII. THE SILKWORM GODDESS

蚕神与

In ancient times, there was a girl who was often left alone by her father, who traveled a lot. She missed him, and joked with her companion the horse, saying, "Horse, if you bring my father home, I'll marry you."

The horse seemed to understand. He broke his tether and galloped away. He ran for days and found her father, who was surprised to see his horse thousands of li from home. Looking in the direction he came from, the horse neighed sorrowfully. The man thought something was wrong and hurried home. His daughter told him she had missed him very much, that the horse had understood her feelings and gone to fetch him.

Happy to have such a smart and sympathetic horse, her father fed him the best fodder, but the horse refused to eat. When the girl passed the stable, he jumped and neighed loudly. When her father asked why the horse behaved so strangely, the girl had to tell him about her broken promise. The father would never let his daughter marry the horse. And before leaving home again, he killed the horse and lay the hide in the sun to dry. A few days later, as the girl sat close by the horse's hide, it suddenly wrapped around her and disappeared with her, as fast as the wind blows.

Heartbroken, he looked everywhere for her. He found a worm wrapped in a cocoon, moving its horselike head, spinning out long, white silk. He knew it was his daughter in the horse's hide, transformed into a silkworm. Henceforth she was known as the Silkworm Goddess. To celebrate the Emperor's victory over Chi You, she presented him with her silk. He ordered that all his clothes be made of silk, and his wife Luo Zhu raised silkworms, soon a major occupation of Chinese women.

XVIII. THE HEADLESS WARRIOR

Xing Tian was an official under the great Yan Emperor of the Sun. When he learned that the Yan emperor had been defeated and was confined to his southern domain, and that Chi You had been killed, he decided to act.

Angrily he rushed into the central court, with a shield in his left hand and an axe in his right hand. On the way he fought through many heavily guarded passes, yet none of the celestial generals could stop him.

The Yellow Emperor, shocked and infuriated, picked up his double-edged sword to meet Xing Tian in combat. They brought the battle down to earth, near Mount Chang Yang, the birthplace of the Yan Emperor, whose memory fueled their hatred all the more. Wielding axe and sword, neither was victorious, until at last the Yellow Emperor won the upper hand, cutting off Xing Tian's head, as big as a small hill. It rolled down to the foot of the mountain.

While Xing Tian was groping for his head on the ground, the Yellow Emperor, aware of his ability to put his head back on again, cut the mountain into two halves. Xing Tian's head was caught in the crevice of the mountain, which closed around it, never to be retrieved.

Xing Tian fought on, headless, using his two breasts as eyes, and his navel as a mouth -- but it was too late. The Yellow Emperor had already returned victorious to the central court of the heavens.

XVIX. ZHUAN XU CUT OFF THE HEAVENLY LADDER

顓頊斷天梯

When the Yellow Emperor tired of being supreme ruler in the heavenly court, he passed his position on to his grandson, Zhuan Xu. For a short time in power, Zhuan Xu showed superior administrative skills. His first important act was to dispatch two of the gods to cut off the route that linked heaven to earth, known as the heavenly ladder.

By way of the heavenly ladder humans had been able to lodge complaints directly with the gods, and the gods would come down to tour the earth. There was no strict barrier between gods and humans. But the god Chi You had taken advantage of the ladder to come down and instigate a rebellion against the Emperor. Those who refused to follow him were massacred. To protect the people, the Yellow Emperor sent down his army and wiped out the rebellion.

When Zhuan Xu inherited the throne from his grandfather, he thought about that war in which so many had died, and decided that easy contacts between gods and humans did more harm than good. So he sent the god Zhong and the god Li to break up the ladder.

The god Zhong stretched his huge arms with all his might to push the sky upward, while the god Li used his powerful arms to press the earth downward. The ladder could no longer reach the ground. Now that the old way of coming down to earth was gone, only occasionally would some god descend to earth, while no earthly being could ascend to heaven. This separation created both order and dissension among humans. Society became hierarchical, as those who wanted to be rulers on earth forced others to be their slaves, and people were often harrassed by their own kinsmen.

XX. GONG GONG KNOCKED DOWN BU ZHOU MOUNTAIN

Zhuan Xu, who had some good ideas, also did a very foolish thing. He bound all the celestial bodies -- the sun, the moon and all the stars -- to the northern part of the sky, interrupting their normal course of motion in the universe. As a result, some places on earth were blindingly bright, others were always dark. The imperious ruler did not care that life had become unbearable for all the people.

The Yan Emperor's grandson, Gong Gong, wanted to restore order to the world. So he gathered all the other gods together in secret, to resist the cruel deity. They fought a war with Zhuan Xu, moving the front line from heaven to the foot of Bu Zhou mountain, a strange mountain, bare of trees and made up of layers and layers of rocks. It had been transformed from one of the tortoises' feet put there by Nü Wa to hold up the sky.

Here the two armies fought on and on. Enraged by the stalemate, Gong Gong, the strongest of the gods, knocked his head against Bu Zhou Mountain, breaking the mountain pillar in half. Echoes resounded, the sky rocked, the earth trembled -- and the sun, moon and stars resumed their normal course in the universe. The land in the southeast caved in to become a huge pit, filling up with the waters flowing from rivers and lakes, to become the Great Sea. And so the cruel Zhuan Xu was defeated.

XXI. CANG XIE INVENTED CHINESE CHARACTERS

The Yellow Emperor, the ancestor of the Han people living in the Yellow River Valley, was credited with the inventions of music and medicine, and even with establishing the civilizations of the Han people in China. The written characters of the Chinese language were invented by one of his officials called Cang Xie.

Cang Xie had a broad dragon-like face with four shining eyes. As a child, he was fond of drawing, and as he grew up his interest in the world around him also grew. He spent hours observing celestial bodies and earthly creatures. He especially loved to muse on the distribution of stars, the configuration of the mountains and rivers, and the texture of the tortoise shell. Based on his observation of these natural phenomena, he created the characters of the Chinese language.

When his characters were first brought to light, it is said that the whole world was shocked, showers of grain poured from the sky, and ghosts cried at night. It was feared people might give up farming and become interested in playing with the characters, and that ghosts were afraid of the power the characters might bring to the people.

sun moon fire water goat horse

XXII. THE COWHERD AND THE WEAVER GIRL

牛郎織女

The Supreme Emperor's granddaughter lived on the east bank of the great Silver River (we call it the Milky Way). With magic silk, she wove beautiful clouds which changed their colors according to the time of day and the season. Her weaving and that of her sisters was used to make celestial clothing.

Right under the Silver River, on the Earth, lived a Cowherd whose parents had died when he was very little. He was cruelly treated by his brother and sister-in-law. Leaving home with only an old cow and his shepherd's flute, he learned to take care of himself. Looking down from heaven, the weaver girl was very sympathetic.

One day his cow began to speak in the human tongue, telling him the celestial weavers were coming to bathe in a nearby river, and that the one whose clothes he could grab would become his wife. At first unbelieving, the cowherd followed the instructions and went to the riverside. He took the weaver girl's clothes; she fell in love and agreed to marry him.

After their marriage, the cowherd tilled the land and the weaver girl wove at home. Soon they had a son and a daughter. But when the Emperor's mother heard about it she was furious, and sent the gods to bring back her wayward granddaughter.

Following closely, the cowherd put his two children in the baskets slung from his shoulder pole. As they approached the Silver River, the Emperor's mother pulled out her golden hairpin to draw a line along the River, which became a raging torrent. The little girl in the front basket suggested scooping up all the water of the river so they could cross it. The Emperor's mother, touched by their devotion, allows them to meet each year on the seventh day of the seventh month.

On that night, many magpies form a bridge over the Silver River. If you look carefully, you can see the family standing on the bridge. On each side of the River is a bright star. One is the Cowherd, the other is the Weaver Girl. On each side of the cowherd at equal distance in a straight line, are two smaller stars, two children sitting in baskets slung from each end of his shoulder pole.

XXIII. KUA FU CHASED THE SUN

夸父追日

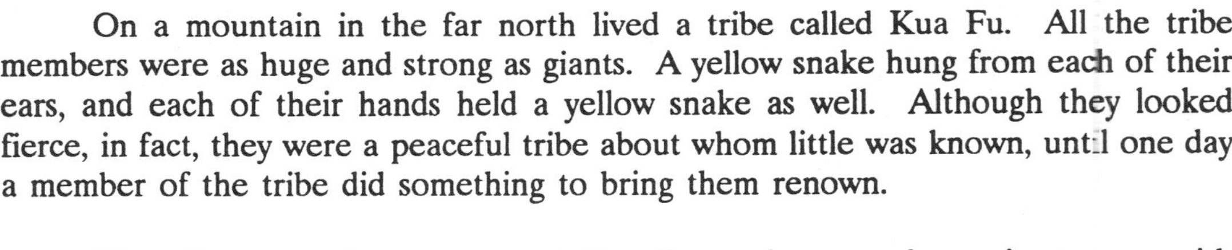

On a mountain in the far north lived a tribe called Kua Fu. All the tribe members were as huge and strong as giants. A yellow snake hung from each of their ears, and each of their hands held a yellow snake as well. Although they looked fierce, in fact, they were a peaceful tribe about whom little was known, until one day a member of the tribe did something to bring them renown.

The tribesman, whose name was Kua Fu, made a grand promise to race with the sun. With giant strides, he chased the falling sun toward the west. He covered a thousand li in a day, following the sun to Gorge Gu, where it rested. Kua Fu was so close to the sun that he stretched out his arms to hold it. But he felt extremely thirsty so close to the blazing sun, and exhausted from running all day, he bent down to drink up all the waters of the Yellow River and the Wei River, in two big gulps.

Still thirsty, he ran to the north to drink from the big lake. But before he could reach the lake, casting aside his walking stick, he fell to the ground like a towering mountain, creating a huge noise throughout the world. He died of thirst and exhaustion.

Where his stick fell, there grows a peach orchard, providing fruit to quench the thirst of later travelers.

XXIV. A FOOLISH OLD MAN TRIED TO MOVE MOUNTAINS

In the northern Mountains lived an old man named Yu Gong (the foolish old man). In front of his home were two mountains, one called Tai Hang, the other Wang Wu, blocking his doorway and causing much inconvenience. So he gathered his family together to see how to remove the mountains.

His practical wife asked how they would dispose of the rocks and dirt. His sons and grandsons said they could dump them into the East Sea. As they all agreed, they began to dig. It took a year to carry one load of rocks to the sea and return home.

An old man living by the river laughed at their stupidity, and said to Yu Gong, "Old man, you are already ninety years old. How can you remove the two mountains?"

Yu Gong replied, "I am old, but my sons will live after me. When they die, my grandsons will live after them. Generation after generation, we will dig into the mountains, until they are gone."

A god overheard their conversation, and fearing the two mountains would be destroyed by Yu Gong, reported to the Emperor of the Heavens, who was touched by the old man's resolve. He sent two gods to carry the mountains away on their backs. Now the mountains Tia Hang and Wang Wu are separate. One can be found in the northeast, the other in the south.

XXV. THE SEVENTH CELESTIAL MAIDEN

七仙女下凡

The youngest of the celestial weavers was called the Seventh Celestial Maiden. Finding life in heaven too dull, she came down to earth without the permission required since her sister had married the cowherd. On her way, she met a young man, Dong Yong, who had sold himself to a local dignitary, Fu, to earn the money needed to pay for the burial of his deceased father. The Seventh Celestial Maid fell in love with him. She invited the earth god to conduct the wedding ceremony, and the Chinese scholar's tree, which grew along the roadside, to be their witness.

Together they went to see the Fu family. After much pleading, Fu agreed that if they could weave ten bolts of silk that night, he would reduce the indenture from three years to one hundred days for both of them. But if they failed, their slavery would be extended for another three years. Although Dong Yong was very worried, the Seventh Celestial Maiden agreed at once.

That night, after she sent her husband to bed, she burnt incense to inform her sisters that she needed help. They came down from heaven, and together produced ten bolts of the most beautiful silk you can be imagine. The next day, they presented the silk to the master, who was indeed very pleased. He let them go free after one hundred days of work. On the way home, his wife informed Dong Yong that she was expecting a child. Overjoyed, they dreamed of future happiness.

When the Emperor found out that the youngest of the celestial maids had married a mortal, he sent a messenger to tell her that if she did not return to heaven at once, Dong Yong would be put to death. She revealed her true identity to her husband, in order to save his life. When he learned the bad news, under the scholartree, he lost consciousness.

Selected bibliography

Joseph Campbell. The Masks of God: Oriental Mythology. NYC: Viking Press, 1962.

Anthony Christie. Chinese Mythology. Library of the World's Myths and Legends. New York: P. Bedrick Books, 1985.

Penelope Farmer, editor. Beginnings. Creation Myths of the World. NYC: Atheneum, 1979.

Yuan Ke (in Chinese). Chinese Myths and Legends. Beijing: Folk Literature Press, 1984.

Chinese names

In China, the family name is followed by the given name(s). The family name of the translator, Li Xiao Ming, is Li; her friends call her Xiao Ming. A title such as "Zi" may be added to the name of a highly respected person like Lao Zi (Lao Tse) or the pottery god, Ning Feng Zi. Women keep their family names, rather than changing them when they are married. Children usually have the father's family name.

Names of persons and places here use the spelling of the Pin Yin system, the standard Romanization of the Chinese language. This is the official language of mainland China and Taiwan, based on the dialects of northern China, with particular reference to the Peking dialect. It is known as Mandarin in western countries.